The Way of Ping

Also by Stuart Avery Gold

Ping: A Frog in Search of a New Pond

Coauthored by Stuart Avery Gold

Success at Life: How to Catch and Live Your Dream

Dragon Spirit: How to Self-Market Your Dream

Tiger Heart, Tiger Mind: How to Empower Your Dream

Wowisms: Words of Wisdom for Dreamers and Doers

The Zentrepreneur's Idea Log & Workbook

The Way of Ping

Journey to the Great Ocean

STUART AVERY GOLD

Newmarket Press
New York

This book is published in the United States of America.

First Edition

ISBN: 978-1-55704-820-2

10 9 8 7 6 5 4 3 2 1

Library of Congress Cataloging-in-Publication Data

Gold, Stuart Avery.
  The way of ping : journey to the great ocean / Stuart Avery Gold. — 1st ed.
      p. cm.
  ISBN 978-1-55704-820-2
  1. Change (Psychology) 2. Adaptability (Psychology) I. Title.
  BF637.C4G646 2009
  158.1—dc22

                                    2008037500

QUANTITY PURCHASES

Companies, professional groups, clubs, and other organizations may qualify for special terms when ordering quantities of this title. For information or a catalog, write Special Sales Department, Newmarket Press, 18 East 48th Street, New York, NY 10017; call (212) 832-3575; fax (212) 832-3629; or e-mail info@newmarketpress.com.

www.pingthebook.com
www.newmarketpress.com

Illustrations © 2009 by Machiko

Manufactured in the United States of America
This book has been printed on acid-free paper.

CONTENTS

For Molly

*A note from the author
about writing the sequel to* Ping

Softly and steadily, *Ping: A Frog in Search of a New Pond* has become an international phenomenon, published in translation around the world, allowing us to circle back together again, and I am grateful. If you are reading this, chances are you took that little book to heart, and blessings to you all. If you haven't read the book, probably some echoes of its existence are the reason that we've become connected. Either way, according to what I've read and heard, the principles and lessons woven throughout the story of *Ping* have become a touchstone for many, and thank you very much. Business managers give copies to their employees, teachers quote it to their students, and readers all over the globe use the frog-found wisdom to help them navigate the daily rapids of challenge and change.

The message that living your best life, the life of your deepest desires, can be attained through a life of choice and action is a truth that screams out to anyone who would quiet themselves enough to listen. To polish the point, people have fallen for Ping. Not alone in that, me too. So Ping returns to share his journey, giving us much more of what matters as the shaping of life wondrously surrounds us. And since on this earth, every writer loves to have company as he follows a good story, here's to you. . . .

With appreciation,

For the enlightened mind,
the Lotus paradise is everywhere.
For those still seeking their truth,
it is found in the tranquillity of the ocean.

1

The Grand Visit

Once upon a place . . .

Most of the pond dwellers began to gather twenty-four hours early. Those who came from the furthermost edges of the pond had arrived some forty hours before that, which was important only if you wanted to grab a good seat. Even the turtles knew that if you wanted a spot up close or if you wanted one in the shade, you were in terrible trouble if you didn't get there in a hurry. The turtles were great believers in a good spot so, as much as they could, they hurried.

Especially lucky were the creatures that arrived early enough to claim a place on the flat rock among the brilliant blue bellflowers, elder blossoms, and fragrant gardenia, for all agreed they truly had a superb view. And hovering above it all, Dragonfly kept a lookout.

There were many wonderful jobs around the pond, but on this day, flitting and dancing around the roof of the world with delicate wings of gauze, Dragonfly had a task that was the envy of all. Having the optimum vantage point, Dragonfly was designated in charge of rumor control.

As the crowd grew, the rumors of Ping's arrival continued to mount, so Dragonfly had the vital task of darting about spreading truth. It was noontime on the dot when Dragonfly announced that Ping's splash time was imminent, then he cleared the air to make way for what could only be described as an extraordinary straight and fine leap of distance, followed by an oh, so colossal and spectacular splash.

Those who were new to Ping's glorious jumping thought, How fantastic, and said so. Those whose memories were full of the stories told said only this: are they ever right. Ping's jumping was much more than a thrill to behold—it was proof that the legend of Ping the frog was pure.

Ping's adventures had become fable, his inner metamorphosis mythical. His transformative journey had brought Ping such notoriety that it wasn't any wonder a large group had amassed for the spectacle of his appearance. Whatever else was to take place at the pond that day, there was no denying that the moment belonged to the honored visitor whose spring-legged leaps of distance they had heard so much about.

Nimbly, Ping pulled himself up onto a lily pad, accepting the hoorays and hazzahs, the waves and endless chants of "Ping, Ping, Ping" caressing his ears. The crowd grew quiet only as it parted way for its ancient ruler, the lordly Toad the Elder.

How long Toad the Elder had held the occupation of ruler, no one knew. It had only come up for conversation once in

*A bigger world could indeed be
found outside their pond.*

recent memory at the annual Bugfest, when Tortoise, who was then 106, remarked that Toad had ruled the pond for as long as he could remember. That was good enough for the rest. The pond dwellers loved tradition.

Whenever Toad the Elder took a break from dozing to totter out and grumpily appear, he was greeted royally and with reverence, for he represented the origin of origins, the deliverer of all that was wise and wonderful.

Toad was from the pond, but his voice was from the clouds. It was weak and wispy, and even the rabbits at the water's edge had to tilt their long ears to catch every word. So whenever Toad the Elder chose to speak, the inhabitants of the pond listened closely. Whatever Toad the Elder said, the inhabitants of the pond believed.

Toad made a gnarled, throat-clearing sound, raised his weakening arms, and with a sweeping gesture said, "Today is a day of salutation for the one who leaps great distances."

Thunderous roar of cheers.

"Welcome to our home, the magnificence of all that exists. The most glorious body of water ever imagined by any living being. From here to there and from there to here, nothing could be more than our pond."

This was a declaration that Toad had stated before and stated often.

"So tell me, Frog, why is it that you have devoted yourself to the jumping that you do?"

"Always to further challenge the sky," Ping impulsively beamed.

Toad glanced imperiously across his subjects and observed the nods and smiles from the younger frogs. More precisely, he took note of a whispering Daikon and Hodo, two of the more troublesome young frogs ever spawned.

Even as tadpoles, Daikon and Hodo had not been easy. Their penchant for venturing out too far from the safety of vegetation in the pond shallows was a constant source of head-shaking among the adult frogs. When the day came that Daikon and Hodo grew into the shape of full-fledged frogs, they found that their affection for each other grew as well. Daikon was sure of one thing: Hodo carried the colors of the world in her perfect, glistening skin. And that was enough for him.

In the whole long history of the pond, no two creatures had enjoyed the close together time that they had spent chatting through the afternoons, their days full, enjoying each other's company, questioning the certainty of their surroundings, and pondering the very nature of their everyday existence. Their inquisitive spirit and rebellious behavior had become an irritation to Toad, and today was no different.

Toad snorted his disapproval at Daikon's and Hodo's brazen glee. There was no understanding the young anymore. He turned away, adjusted his royal robes. "So,

What is greatly dreamed is nobly dared.

then, from where is it that you have come to visit us?" he asked Ping.

"From the Great Ocean."

Bewildered silence from one and all.

A puzzled look clouded Toad's old eyes. "Hmmm. I've never heard of such a place," he said. "But do not be overwhelmed by our most marvelous pond. How much smaller is your ocean?"

"As with all things, Highness, the ocean should not be judged by its size but by its openness," Ping replied simply.

"Nonsense." Toad made a show of proudly pointing out their surroundings. "How many of your oceans would it take to fill our pond?"

"With respect, I am delighted to tell you that the ocean is a vast thing."

"What do you mean, exactly? Do you mean to say that the ocean can't even begin to compare?"

Ping nodded. "It is true, there is no comparison."

"As I thought," Toad said, looking to his subjects. "But still, how small is the ocean?"

"The ocean is not small; it is big."

"Big? Big how? Is it half as big as our pond?"

Ping shook his head. "No. Bigger."

The crowd began to stir.

The grouping of young frogs blinked in amazement.

Toad began to ponder the absurdity of the statement. "Is it as big as our pond?" His voice was growing stronger.

"Bigger still. I guarantee you," Ping answered. "All rivers pour into it, yet it never overflows. It is constantly being drained, yet it never empties. The seasons of spring and winter bring no change. Floods and droughts also leave it unchanged. It is vastly superior to both stream and pond. Majesty, forgive me. I don't mean to displease you, but your pond would not even be a drop in the Great Ocean."

The crowd gasped and looked to Toad the Elder.

Toad the Elder glared at Ping and boomed angrily, "What kind of creature is this that visits us with such lies?" Toad had been tough when he was younger, and he was still tough. "You speak heresy!"

"I speak the truth," Ping replied.

"I promise you here and now that there is nothing bigger, nothing more exciting, and nothing more fulfilling than our pond!"

Ping blinked, blinked again. His remarkable eyes looked at Toad as if he had the power to see through him, which he did. With a voice that could only be described as calm, he invited Toad and all who would be willing to have both the courage and the curiosity to take the journey of discovery, to follow him and see for themselves how glorious and true the Great Ocean was, that a bigger world could indeed be found outside their pond.

No one ever dared disagree with Toad. His ancient face began to flush, his eyes blazed with fire. "SUCH INSOLENCE!" Toad bellowed furiously, sputtering spittle. "YOU

INVITE ME TO SEE THE OCEAN TO TEACH ME, AS IF I DON'T HAVE ANY KNOWLEDGE OR WISDOM? THERE IS NOTHING CALLED OCEAN. THERE IS NOTHING BEYOND THE BEYOND. . . . " Toad the Elder continued the tirade without even taking a breath, his voice strengthening and reverberating as his rage increased. While his words hit Ping head-on, it should be noted, so did the bog balls. The older pond dwellers had begun hurling bog balls at Ping, quickly fashioning handfuls of muck and marsh into spherical scatter splatters that pelted Ping from this way and that as they joined in Toad's roaring rage, fuming, screaming at Ping to leave their pond for good. Some of the bog balls reached their target with remarkable force and accuracy.

Furor...

Or, to be more specific, fury. And why Ping did not leap away was not only a good question, clearly, it was the only question. Ping stood his ground, blinked and winced and blinked some more, taking the jeers and sneers and the bruising blows of the bog balls, knowing that how you respond to others is always more important than how they respond to you.

Finally, looking out at the youngest faces of the smallest pond dwellers, Ping said, "What is greatly dreamed is nobly dared. . . . The journey begins with you." Then Ping jumped as straight and as fine a jump as he had ever jumped, disappearing from sight, far into the heavenly distance, gone.

The older creatures, satisfied, shouted yes! Two of the younger creatures marveled with exuberance and very bravely shouted yes! also.

None at the pond knew it then, but history was about to be created.

2

Old Path, New Path

They agreed to meet at midnight, under the ten thousand stars, in the thicket of reed grass. "Meet" was probably the wrong word. "Hide" would be more correct, given that gathering together in secrecy was against Toad the Elder's latest decrees. Since Ping's visit, old Toad had been keeping a very suspicious eye on the young frogs. Most, of course, did as they were told. Six small frogs, led by Daikon and Hodo, did not.

"We must be careful to stifle our voices as we go," Daikon cautioned, making certain that his own voice was speaking softly in the night. "Remember how sound travels over water."

The six small hoplings looked at one another. Trembling. No one said anything for a moment because all of their terrible fears dealt with leaving the pond's haven of security and familiarity for the unknown. It was Kiku, the greenest of the group, who spoke all their thoughts then.

"It is so, so very nice here, isn't it?" Kiku said to Daikon, thinking of their pond, their world. "What if this is as good as it is?"

For a moment, there was a silence. Daikon nodded his head with heartbreaking understanding. He had known that when the time came, his fellow frogs might be afraid to leave the comfort of their pond for possibility. He could not fault them. Still, could depriving oneself of possibility be anything but sad?

Daikon took a long pause, and then started speaking. "We are all creators of our own dreams, and we make our own decisions. You must do what you believe in," he said.

Kiku, though he smiled, could not stop his sudden tears. "You'll be killed out there. You know that."

"Maybe."

"Please don't go."

There was no changing Daikon's mind. Seeing this, Kiku held out his hand, offering Daikon a necklace fashioned from a single root vine with a pond stone as a pendant. "To remember us," said Kiku.

Daikon put on the necklace, looked at the pendant, then gazed at the group, his turn now to be emotional. "I will not forget any of you," he said. "This I promise."

Hodo made a little nod, found it very hard to breathe. There had not been an evening that the dream of leaving the pond did not flutter behind her sleepy eyelids, and now it was time.

Tears.

The small frogs sat silent then, the six. They did what they could, smiled sad, brave smiles at Daikon and Hodo. Who reassuring-

You must do what you believe in.

ly smiled back. The evening could not have been prettier, the breezes inviting and warm.

Daikon and Hodo looked up at the twinkling stars, then at their fellow froglings, giving them an affirmative blink, embracing each.

And with that, took a leap of faith into the beckoning darkness, their own belief never more evident.

3

The Corridor of
Useless Trees

The Corridor of Useless Trees was, of course, entirely misnamed. As to why this was, no one knows, though most likely the sheer number of crooked and twisted trees that shadowed the ground could have been the reason.

Those who would travel the corridor saw the old trees as too crooked, twisted, and knotty to be of any use to carpenter or carver, the trunks and branches so gnarled it was thought that the trees served no purpose at all.

Thus, for generations the Corridor of Useless Trees stood undisturbed, never cut down, as if the majestic, giant trees seemed to know that their uselessness was the very thing that made them perfect for birds and animals, providing a cheery place for them to dwell in peace.

It was here, drawn by the seclusion of the bough shade, that Ping sat in studied silence, embracing the poetry of form that the tree shadows cast. As had been his practice for years, Ping faithfully spent many hours of the day training his mind, learning its ways, penetrating into the essence of his true nature, opening himself to new insights, vistas, and possibilities.

Breathing in breezes laden with the scent of distant mountain cherry blossoms, Ping happily contemplated the inner landscape of a settled mind. He was sitting there in deep and steady concentration when, at long last, Daikon and Hodo excitedly spied him, dimly visible in the distance.

The hopeful hoppers squinted to make sure. Their eyes did not deceive. Happy and awed, they quietly hopped forward as close as they dared.

"Shhh . . . he's sleeping," whispered Hodo.

Daikon watchfully moved in a little closer, close enough to examine Ping's still face a moment more. What he observed was most strange. "He looks like he's sleeping, but I don't think he is."

The two young frogs stared.

Ping, darkened by shadow, opened his eyes a peek's worth, closed them again.

Hodo and Daikon exchanged a quizzical glance.

"I'm meditating," Ping said then, startling the wee frogs and causing them to lose their balance.

Hodo and Daikon regained their footing and looked at Ping somewhat strangely. Exchanged head nods. In unison they managed a quick, "I get it. I get it."

That was all they ever answered. "I get it. I get it." Sun leaves, moon comes. "I get it. I get it." Moon leaves, sun comes. "I get it. I get it."

Of course they didn't, but whenever young frogs are befuddled by something beyond thought, which is really most of the

*Why are we always more ready to believe
in what's outside of us than what's inside?*

time, they instinctively answer, "I get it." Words they say loud and words they say often.

This habit begins at an early age. They start out as pollywogs, go through early life swimmingly well, then wake up one morning losing their tails, growing arms and legs, asking what happened. Even though they find the explanation unfathomable, they immediately say, "I get it." They repeat the phrase continually in their desperate need to convince themselves that indeed they do.

Since the earliest time, frogs have confused understanding for realization and realization for liberation. Even today, at bogs, marshes, ponds, and lakes across the world, the practice continues, although the croaking of "I get it ... I get it" is mistakenly heard as "ribbit ... ribbit." Such is the uncertainty of a young frog's mind. An uncertainty that Ping, once a young froglet himself, well understood.

Ping took a deep, relaxing breath. Another. Examined the young frogs before him. The marsh mist was rising as he began to explain: "Meditation is the stillness within us all, where the truth of the heart surrounds the mind. It is stillness that harmonizes the body and mind to recognize the limitless possibility that exists for each of us. Strengthening the body is done by bringing it to move. Strengthening the mind is done by bringing it to rest. Through meditation you discover that while it is the brain that moves the body, it is the mind that moves the world."

Shrug. "I get it. I get it." Hodo and Daikon hadn't the least idea.

"Clearly," said Ping, barely suppressing his smile.

Ping then opened his eyes, and in quietude hopped a few hops. A trifle hungry, he checked the ground for squirmies to eat.

Hodo was very nervous being in Ping's presence. She looked up at the dense canopy of twisted branches. "Is it here among the useless trees that you spend your time?" she managed to ask.

"Always there is a drama about the useless and the useful," Ping said as he spotted a crawly to swallow. "The woodworker sees these trees as useless, but do not the same trees provide inspirational sweeping strokes of beauty for the painter's brush? For all things there is a unique purpose. For each and every one of us, a reason for being. Perhaps it is your wondering about your own purpose that brings you from the pond?"

The two small frogs looked at each other. All their lives they had been told that never in this world had a wisdom existed beyond that of Toad the Elder, yet Ping's great intellect was totally in evidence now.

Daikon could scarcely get his words out: "For some time now, we have battled with our restlessness. As we grew, so did our hopes and dreams. We believed that our boring world could not be the only world. That there was something bigger for us to experience. We have spent our days with only the belief that some dawn we would discover something more."

"To believe that something must be is one thing, but to do what it takes to experience it is another," said Ping.

"Your visit soared our spirits," Hodo said. "Suddenly, for Daikon and me, everything at the pond was without reason—there was nothing for us remaining there. This is why we have traveled to find you."

"Nonsense," Ping said then. "One who becomes filled with such suchness travels to find himself. For the branch to move, it must feel the wind. It is the freshness of the wind that causes your doubts to drop like the autumn leaves and urges you to follow your bliss."

Hodo began to grow excited. She gave Daikon a nudge. "Tell him," she said then.

"It is our only dream to go to the Great Ocean and find happiness," Daikon declared. "Please say you will show us the way."

"Why are we always more ready to believe in what's outside of us than what's inside?" asked Ping. "There is no way to happiness; happiness is the Way." He contemplated a moment, then picked up a stick and etched the word "Way" in the dirt, glanced back. Said nothing.

A confused Daikon and Hodo looked at what was written, tussled with the meaning.

Ping again scribed the word "Way" in the dirt.

Daikon and Hodo took a hop nearer.

Hodo furled her brow. "What is the Way?" she asked.

"The Way is your daily life," Ping replied. "It is awakening your mind and seeing your true nature. It is letting go of the attitudes and expectations of others so that you may enter the stream of your own destiny, flowing with the wellspring of all possibility. It is a life that, sunny or cloudy, brings joy to your days. A life where you do what you like and like what you do by being who you are and not what others have dictated. The Way does not ask us to be what we are not, but to be more fully what we are.

"By focusing on your deepest hopes and aspirations, you not only discover the starting point of your life, but the source of it, your inborn reason, the life you were born to live. Every living thing has a place in the natural order of things, with a destiny to fulfill. Let everything be what it naturally is and the Way occurs."

Ping took a step forward and said, "All the fish needs to do is get lost in the water. All the frog needs to do is get lost in the Way. Flowing with, not fighting against your instincts, your desires, for the flow knows where to go.

"But also be awake to the fact that within the Way there always exists two paths, the path of what is and the path of what can be. Through the choices you make and the actions you take, you can travel the path or not. It is up to you."

Memories flooded Ping. Remembering his own lessons, he felt that what he said next would have made his old masterful mentor beam and nod in appreciation. "To leap at life's boundless opportunities, you must do in order to be."

Hodo and Daikon knew none of this, but hearing it made them happier than ever before. Such true wisdom, such truer guidance. With expanding imaginations and their faces lit with hope, they looked up at the vibrantly full sunset, evening fire trails of purple and scarlet flooding the sky. With her fingers very much crossed, Hodo asked, "Is it too late to get started?"

There was a long pause. Then Ping said these wonderful words: "It is never too late to be what you can become."

The sunset went golden.

4

The Awakened Eye Sees No Obstacles

For the next two days, Ping led Hodo and Daikon through many miles of boulders and basins. Some of the rocks of the mountain path became more and more of a challenge for the small frogs to jump over.

"I had no idea that our traveling would take so long or be so difficult," panted Hodo, who was having a terrible time keeping up. She was glazed with fatigue and began to believe that she might lack the strength to persevere. "How far is the Great Ocean?" she asked.

"Your greatest life is always right in front of you," Ping answered.

Hodo looked ahead, tried to make her eyes focus. "Maybe the boulders are blocking our view," she said to Daikon, trying to figure it out. "But I tell you now, these are easily the biggest rocks I have ever seen."

Daikon agreed: "There's no denying it— to jump such sky-toppers is surely too much of an obstacle."

"The only real obstacle on your path to possibility will always be yourself," Ping said. "Too often we do not see things as they are; we see things as we are."

Ping stopped to allow his young followers to rest under the long shadow of a large looming boulder. "Spend little or no time dwelling on what you can't do and instead think entirely in terms of what you can and must do," said Ping. "A boulder may block the path but never the Way. No adversity, difficulty, or doubt can have any power over you unless you allow it.

"The two most important rules of the Way are to begin and to continue. The Way never concerns itself with what we do not have, do not want, or cannot do. It only sustains what we do have, do want, and can do. You must always strive to find your own footing. Whatever the problems or challenges you face, know that you have the capacity to master and surmount them.

"A jumping frog is not the only creature to experience life's ups and downs. Discouragement and setbacks are part of every traveler's tale. To live the life you deserve, you must believe that what you have on the inside can rise above any obstacle or circumstance on the outside. Believe and you will achieve."

"I get it. I get it," from Daikon and Hodo.

"I doubt that somehow," from Ping.

Then, summoning all the energy they could summon, both Daikon and Hodo started jumping into the air, leaping as high and as mightily as they could, attempting to clear the mammoth boulder in order to get to the other side.

No chance.

Ping watched, shaking his head. The fact was that the boulder was so massive that not even he, the greatest jumping wonder the world had ever known, could hope to clear it.

Knowing this and more, Ping surveyed the boulder. Then he set to work, expertly hopping onto the tier of rock formations that edged the boulder's side, bounding his way in an upward direction. He had already reached the boulder's plateau by the time Daikon and Hodo collapsed on the ground, exhausted, puffing from their efforts.

"Waiting for you," Ping called, looking down.

Hodo and Daikon gazed up in bewilderment. They had jumped their lungs out and their legs. How was it that Ping was there above them? Somehow, in some miraculous way, Ping had not been denied by the wall of stone.

"We thought that the only way to conquer the boulder was to go over it," Daikon breathlessly managed.

"Commendable determination, I must admit," Ping said. "But where you saw a stopping boulder, I saw a stepping stone. The path of reality is the one most often overlooked. Know that every problem that exists outside of us has its solution inside of us. Work in harmony with life's circumstances. Be aware of your ability to correct your course and move onward. To change your life you must be willing to change your mind. Alternative options can be hidden by an unwillingness to listen or an unwillingness to see. Greet challenge with change; see it with new eyes. When you change the way you look at things, the things you look at change."

Daikon knew a lesson when he heard one. He also knew that Hodo was too weak and too weary to continue. Hodo was a fine and fit jumper, but the attempts at storming the boulder had left her terribly ashen, drained of all the colors of the world.

"Go on without me . . . ," Hodo panted and sagged, closing her faithful eyes.

The rise to success is achieved by lifting others.

What a terrible moment! Daikon saw the helplessness in her face and didn't know what to do. Distressed, he looked at his dear diminishing Hodo, the glory of her perfectly colored skin perfect no more. Daikon glanced up at Ping. "How can I help Hodo?"

"By helping yourself," Ping instructed.

"How can I help myself?"

"By helping someone else," said Ping.

"By helping to change the circumstances of another life, yours will change, too," Ping explained. "The rise to success is achieved by lifting others. A great part of the journey is who you choose to travel the path with. Being a compassionate companion, knowing that you can depend on a friend and be dependable for them, through adventure and hardship, is one of the grand gifts of our existence. How you treat such trueness is one of life's most personal of moral tests."

Daikon nodded, then turned to Hodo and stroked her cheek lightly with his hand.

When she looked up at him, he gave her his best smile and nodded that all was going to be well. "Hop on my back," he commanded. "We'll go up together."

With that, they did.

Slowly, with great effort. Not the easiest task, as Hodo clung to Daikon's neck and Daikon summoned all his remaining strength and gallantly scaled the rock, finding a crevice for his hands, another for his feet, and then another and another as he carefully climbed.

That's how Daikon mounted the steep side of the boulder and then maneuvered his way cautiously down the other side to sanctuary, once again joining Ping, who sat in an open space facing the bamboo frontier, waiting patiently to continue their teachings.

5

Bamboo Teachings

Light from the wedge of the moon dusted the rustling wooded stems of the lush green grove.

"Quiet . . . ," Ping whispered, a finger to his lips.

Hodo and Daikon immediately hushed.

"What is it?" Daikon wondered.

"Listen," said Ping with great care. "Listen to the inspirational sermons of the bamboo. Awaken yourselves to how strong and clear a voice it has as it sways and dances in the breeze of life. Make the most of its significance. Pay attention to the silence between the bamboos clacking, for it speaks divine wisdom to those who would be quiet enough to listen."

Puzzled, Hodo and Daikon listened very hard for a moment.

Nothing.

"How is it that you hear these things?" Hodo asked.

"How is it that you do not?" Ping replied.

Hodo looked to Daikon; they hadn't the least idea what Ping was talking about. "We don't understand," said Daikon. "Maybe you need to help us straighten things out."

"Too much energy is spent trying to straighten things out, when the secret to overcoming obstacles and challenge is to bend. Learn to follow the way of bamboo. Bamboo works in harmony with nature, remaining flexible in its response to external conditions. While the strongest tree can be uprooted and knocked over in a storm, bamboo prevails in adverse conditions by bending and yielding to the prevailing winds.

"You too must remain flexible and responsive to unpredictable circumstances when they appear. Learn to listen newly. By remaining flexible, you allow things to speak to you and tell you what to do with them.

"As you have experienced, there will always be more than enough obstacles that will block your path. Life will see to that. The cloud of disappointment, rejection, frustration, and failure looms over you every time you set out. Do not count on clearing skies. Be like bamboo, which is strong, resilient, and unbreakable. By mirroring the resilience of bamboo you will be able to sustain yourself against staggering setbacks, unfair reversals, and resounding defeats.

"Success and happiness are yours when you adapt behavior patterns that are flexible in dealing with the many unknowns and changes as they present themselves. The wise frog makes more opportunities than he finds."

Hodo and Daikon nodded. "You have our commitment that we will take this teaching to heart," said Daikon.

"Your commitment to me is nothing. Your commitment to yourself is everything," Ping answered. "All that is necessary for success or failure is contained within the self."

Ping studied their faces. "No one can deliver you a rainbow; it is you who must take on the responsibility to do what you want to do and be what you want to be. Obstacles are there to prevent you. Distractions are there to pull you. Fear is there to keep you where you are. These things will become visible only when you take your eyes off the path. To live your dream, do not worry about what to do—just do what needs to be done. It is decisions, not conditions, that determine your destiny. Travel with no thought in your heart but to do and to be."

"It has not been easy," Daikon said. "Even though we saw what everybody else saw, we thought about things that nobody else thought. No matter how far we believed we could jump, there were those who would say we could not."

"If you believe in yourself, do you need the belief of others?" asked Ping.

"Do not put up with those who would put you down. Distance yourself from those who try to tempt you away from your path and crush your character. Just as birds of a feather flock together, creatures of confidence cluster. They support and encourage others. Attach yourself to those kindred spirits who have faith in who you are and what you desire to accomplish. Inherit their passion for possibility, personal growth, and intention. Intention transforms reality."

"I get it. I get it."

"You can and you must," urged Ping. "The path to fulfillment is not smooth and uneventful. Rather, it is a journey full of doubts and difficulties that will take you to places and times where you will be forced to confront the great unknown. The brave frog leaps beyond what is, into an exhilarating world of what can be."

Again, "I get it. I get it," from Daikon and Hodo.

"We will see," said Ping. "We will see . . ."

Weeks passed.

*If you believe in yourself, do
you need the belief of others?*

Months followed.

This was before calendars, of course, but Ping could tell by the rise and fall of the sun each day, the cycle of the moon each month, that half a year had been spent at the entrance to the bamboo frontier.

For those six months, Ping instructed Daikon and Hodo how to climb up tall shoots of bamboo and climb down tall shoots of bamboo. Each day they climbed a shoot taller than the one they had climbed the day before, Ping explaining that the journey ahead required strengthening body and mastering mind. "To climb successfully, you must climb with your mind, not your arms and legs. To climb successfully, you must have focus. To climb successfully, you must understand that climbing is simply supporting right effort and right mindfulness. To climb successfully, you must climb with ease. You must always strive to reach new levels of competency, strength, and understanding," Ping said simply. "Nature gives every bird its worm, but does not throw it into the nest. A dream is something you go after. Now climb."

They climbed.

Again and again.

Every dawning for six months, Daikon and Hodo scaled a clump of taller and taller bamboo, picking up their pace, honing their skills, and just when they thought there could be on this earth no taller bamboo for them to climb, Ping led them to the tallest one that gated the bamboo frontier, a dense thicket of towering hundred-foot-high shoots.

Looking up, Hodo and Daikon could see no end to the rising columns of the hundred-foot-high bamboo. They had no idea if Ping had brought them there to bear witness to its dramatic height; they only knew that if they were there to challenge its loftiness, clearly there was desperate need for some discussion.

Hodo gulped, her eyes going to the sky. Climbing bamboo was tough enough, but bamboo this high was impossible and she said so.

Daikon wasn't sure.

"Nothing is impossible to a willing mind," Ping decreed. "Like turning your head this way and that, you can turn your mind whichever way you want. As with all things, it's not what you are that holds you back, it's what you think you are not that keeps you in place.

"The months of training have made you both excellent climbers, but it is your mind that requires further polishing. Fuse both body and mind to accomplish your goals and aspirations. Again, we need only the lessons of the bamboo."

There was a pause.

Daikon and Hodo sat, waited for the lesson.

Ping sat quietly, waited for Daikon and Hodo to do what they had to try to do—

Correction: Ping sat quietly, waited for Daikon and Hodo to do what they *had to do*, which was climb to the top of the hundred-foot-high bamboo.

It was inconceivable, of course. For Hodo and Daikon, no word had yet been invented for their apprehension toward climbing such altitude.

Ping turned to his fellow frogs. "The energy that allows the bamboo to grow to such height is the same energy that allows us to grow," he said. "It's within us and around us. We are not separate from it; we are *of* it. To direct our energy is to direct our destiny." Ping pointed toward the hundred-foot-high shoots. "Begin your climb."

"What if we can't make it to the top?" Hodo asked.

"The process of climbing is what matters," answered Ping. "Too often we are easily discouraged when we start looking too far ahead, thinking the commitment too great, the climb too high, so we do not start. Try not to look any farther or commit to anything greater than taking the one step. The one step changes everything. When we have taken the one step, we can look and commit to taking another. Soon we have climbed fifty feet. Soon we have climbed one hundred feet. Soon we have seen the effort through."

Hodo looked up at the tall shoot in front of her, such was her doubt. She sat there, head straight back, staring into the darkness toward the top, before she said, "I have climbed bamboo enough now to know this would be a difficult climb—too lofty a goal."

"The higher the goal, the more difficult the climb," said Ping. "Too lofty or not, only you can decide."

Daikon and Hodo nodded. "What good fortune it is that we have you for a role model," said Hodo.

"Do not entrust your mind to a role model," Ping instructed. "Such speakers are guests from outside the gate. Instead seek out the authenticity of a goal model, an authentic someone who has broken through the gate of mystery to reach the marvelous."

Then, recalling a lesson of his own, Ping said these words: "Attitude equals altitude."

He could have said more, but instead jumped on to a shoot of the hundred-foot-high bamboo and, straight and sure, began climbing with incredible proficiency, zooming quickly, deftly arriving at the top.

Looking up, Daikon and Hodo watched Ping with astonishment. Then they were moving, beginning their own climb up the hundred-foot-high bamboo.

Hand over hand, reaching and grabbing, then reaching and grabbing some more. Both Daikon and Hodo keen on proving themselves to Ping, who was staring down at their progress as he waited for them to reach him. With only the very real possibility of falling their constant companion, Daikon and Hodo continued to climb slowly ever upward.

Up, up.

And, of course, what Ping had said was only too true. The climb became more and more difficult the higher Daikon and Hodo moved, the evening dew making the bamboo slippery, the balmy winds plucking their bodies, their hands and feet beginning to cramp . . . and how high were they now? Daikon wondered. But he didn't wonder for long, as he lost his grip and quickly slid down a few feet before locking his grasp again to stop his descent. Gripping tightly, he peered briefly over his shoulder to the earth below, then at Hodo. She was holding on perfectly steadily, except for her heart, which was trilling inside her ribcage.

"Nice night for a climb," Daikon said when he could finally breathe easily again. Hodo, not about to agree, found certain comfort in knowing that no matter how challenging the climb, only a fall to death could make it any worse. Daikon and Hodo gathered their courage again, then staunchly climbed on.

And on.

Climbing slowly, yes, but climbing. The bamboo swaying by this time more than it ever had in any wind. But Daikon and Hodo paid no attention to its movement. They were also not paying attention to how their arms and legs ached, giving themselves no rest, the distance between them and the top of the hundred-foot-high bamboo beginning to close, their focus so strong, their worries and anxieties in retreat, their confidence increasing with every reach and pull along the way.

Thirty-three feet to go.

Now thirty-two.

They were visibly pleased when they finally, safely, made the full sheer height of the hundred-foot-high bamboo. Clinging to the top of the wind-swaying stalk, getting their breath back, they surveyed the ground beneath, savoring their accomplishment.

Perched from his position, Ping let them enjoy their moment of exultation.

But not for long.

"Keep climbing," Ping instructed.

"Huh?" A confused Daikon looked at Hodo, not sure he heard right. "How do we keep climbing from the top?" he asked Ping.

"Whatever you want to have, do, or be is within your reach when you advance one step further by not holding on."

Daikon and Hodo gripped the tip of what was left of the bamboo more firmly, confused.

Ping did his best to explain. "The things we accomplish have no permanence, only peaks, and we must not stay there. We must always go beyond them," said Ping. "When we let go of all meaning, only what is truly important becomes meaningful. By letting go of things as they are, we can experience things as they might be. Unattached action is action that invites your future. To receive the natural abundance of the Way, we must learn to let go of attachments that keep us from experiencing it. Walk the path that has no end. Dedicate yourself to always going one step further."

Daikon was perplexed and said so. "How are we to climb when we have nothing to grasp?"

"Nothing but empty hands," Ping answered right back.

"What do you mean by 'empty hands'?"

"Empty-handed we entered the world. Through daily living this original simple lesson is lost. Too often our hands are full, filled with tasks, problems, possessions, and decisions that seem impossible to let go of. When events do not go as we would wish, or do go as we wish, we start to grasp and hold on. We must learn how to stop clinging. When our hands become empty, our minds become empty, too. Only then can both our hands and minds be open to the new possibilities that are always present for us."

It was inconceivable, of course. Daikon and Hodo were admittedly frightened. The whole notion of letting go was unthinkable. After all, down was down, always something to bear in mind with a hundred-foot drop and nothing but the hard ground beneath to stop the fall.

Hodo tried a smile and asked if Ping would mind if they thought about what he had instructed them to do.

He minded.

"Like the beauty of a blossom, make going one step further ordinary activity. Take advantage of the energy that drives the dance of life. Holding on will only hold you back. Step lively! Again, you must do in order to be."

And with that, Ping gave a smile to Daikon and Hodo, let go, and fell far across into the night, disappearing amid the emerald leaves of the bamboo branches below.

Whoosh. . . .

Hodo and Daikon looked down, then at each other. Maybe if they were very, very lucky.

Taking a deep breath for courage, Daikon closed his eyes for a contemplative moment, cleared his mind of everything, and then, with his head held high, did a brave thing.

Holding on will only hold you back.

He let go.

Hodo followed.

Whoosh . . . Whoosh . . .

Together they found themselves leaping into a place where too few of us are determined enough to visit: the unbounded, limitless possibility of the everyday world.

Offering no resistance to life, Daikon and Hodo opened themselves up to the ineffable grace and ease of being, the welcoming air carrying them far beyond any boundaries their jumping ever could. Farther and farther they flew onward, from the clutch of their limited thinking to their own limitless potential. For Daikon and Hodo, it was an experience as resplendent as their decision to undertake it.

For Ping it was the greatest gift he could ever have given them: the power to transport them beyond the boundaries of themselves, the innate ability to transcend the realm of ordinary reality to soar the landscape of their own best self.

Seconds later they were all together again, the three of them sitting surrounded by the long night shadows of towering shoots. For Daikon and Hodo, the truth of the moment was beyond their frog reckoning.

"It's hard to believe," Hodo said.

"Being is believing," Ping stated. "The greater the doubt, the greater the awakening. Know now that all doubt arises because of mind. If mind is truly transformed, can doubt remain?"

"You mean, we shouldn't let uncertainty guide us?" asked Hodo.

"Uncertainty is the always. If we stop clinging to the illusion of certainty and trust the uncertainty, the uncertainty will lead us. We must learn to take risks, embrace the uncertainties of our individual lives, of our world. Not allowing the uncertainties to shake us, to paralyze us, to persuade us, to fill us with doubt of our own capability."

"I get it. I get it," from Daikon and Hodo.

"I can only hope," said Ping. "For in order for us to reach the Great Ocean, we now must make an uncertain journey through the myth and nightmare of the bamboo frontier."

"What awaits us in there?" Hodo asked with wary concern.

"Only what you bring with you," Ping answered. Then without hesitation, he headed into the foreboding darkness of the bamboo frontier, with Daikon and Hodo following very close behind.

6

Slither Swamp

Total blackness.

As they pushed deeper into the bamboo frontier, the night in front of them became blacker than the night above, and why that was Daikon and Hodo could not figure for sure. Whatever the reason, the moon was not going along to light the way. They did their best to focus through the eerie darkness, blindly keeping their hops short and guarded. There was no denying that an ominous dread spooked the air. A shaking Hodo could feel the panic starting inside her, and above her heartbeat whispered, "It's either very dark in here or I'm very frightened."

"Very all both, I think," Daikon whispered back, doing his best to stay confident.

"The space between the bamboo is the truth—all else is shadow," said Ping.

"The first enemy of a frog is fear. A horrible enemy, fear adds to darkness, blotting out the wonder and light that shines on your true path of purpose and success. Fear waits hidden from view at every turn, defeating more frogs than any single thing. And if the frog, terrified in its presence, panics and bounds away, it is fear itself that puts an end to his goals and dreams."

Ping turned to Daikon and Hodo. "Fear can make us flee or make us free. It can be defeating or defeated. Once you have placed yourself inside fear, there doesn't seem to be any way to ever get out again, until you discover that it has been brought into existence by your own thought and does not exist outside your own thought. To flourish, know your fears. To truly flourish, rid yourself of your fears.

"Be courageous in your life and in your pursuit of the things you want and what it is you want to become. You must do in order to master the circumstances of life, or risk having the circumstances of life master you.

"No matter what the darkness, never fear the Way, fear only straying from it. For the Way is the path of strength. If you believe in its strength, you will be given the strength. Abandon the Way and all that it can offer will abandon you. Always possess the courage to continue the journey, even if you are scared to pieces."

"What a wonderful lesson," Daikon said, trying to put the best possible light on the situation. "I will remember it in the future."

"You will do well to remember it now," Ping advised, checking their surroundings. "More than you can possibly imagine. Only a reservoir of absolute, unconditional courage will help you tread through what lies ahead: the terror of the swamp where the dead leave no bones."

*Never lose sight of what you
desire or where you wish to be.*

"I don't think I like the sound of such a place," Daikon confessed.

"To contend with Slither Swamp, courage must be your armor," Ping said in a voice that was as steady as steady could be. "More than moonlight and shadow, it's the absence of a will and willingness that will block your path. Never lose sight of what you desire or where you wish to be. Hang on to your idealism, hold fast to your dreams."

Ping continued to lead the way. Off in the distance, a glint of lightning and then something thrashing in shallow water.

For her part, Hodo felt a pulsing panic. In spite of her fear, she tried very hard to do exactly what she was told. Following Ping's words, she called on her courage, but became distracted by what was suddenly closing in on her, a strangeness. Odd. She opened her nostrils wide. She had never encountered such an odor. "That's peculiar."

Daikon also sniffed the dark air, the stench of something foul becoming pungently evident. "Woo-wee. What is that smell?" Daikon asked.

"Woo-wee. What is that smell?" Hodo repeated.

Using his nose now, Ping knew that something very bad was in the offing, that there was evil moving among them, the punishing stench encasing the senses. His eyes darted left and right with great caution. "Snake breath," he warned.

"Snake breath?" Daikon asked, his stomach knotting.

"Hissers and spitters," said Ping, picking up the pace. Don't let them stop you or even slow you down."

Daikon and Hodo had never heard the words before. "Hissers and spitters?" from Daikon as they moved.

"Pressure poisoners," Ping said right back. "Those who will try to pull you from the path of your purpose—your individual wants, goals, and dreams.

"Beware the dream killers that lurk here, imagination crushers there, the wish stranglers in between that can appear in the way of your ultimate calling. Do not let the pressure of doubt and discouragement determine your fate. There are no other creatures that can kill a destiny so silently. Focus on what you want for yourself. Use the commitment of your own reality to confront the conflict and confusion of others. Persistence overcomes resistance. The only way to get through them is to go through them. Stay brave."

This was all that Ping said, because at that very moment, he needed his ears as he listened in the darkness, suddenly hearing the breath sounds. Peering into the unfathomable blackness, he immediately felt movement closing toward them, and that was all he had to know now.

"Something is here. Something is here," Hodo told them, turning to look behind.

"In your seeing, there should be only seeing; in your hearing, nothing but hearing; in your knowing, nothing but knowing. Be guided by what you feel. Clarity is more than a point before your eyes. It is true power."

Hodo looked around for a long moment and that was moment enough. Frightened, she instinctively whirled back to Ping for further reassurance, but found herself facing a reality more frightening than any. Ping was not there. Daikon was not there, either.

Hodo was alone.

Suddenly. Totally. For the first and only time, alone.

Except for the breath sounds, which she could clearly hear starting to surround her.

Hodo opened her eyes wide with the realization and cried out in the night for Daikon, then a cry for Ping. Nothing. Only slither sounds ruling the dark. Daikon and Ping were gone.

Hodo froze.

In horrific panic she knew what she wanted most to do: bolt into a jump and flee back to the safety and security of all her yesterdays. This is what happens when confronted with a new world, a world that challenges with the pall of agony, fear, uncertainty, and doubt. But then Hodo's mind went to Daikon, her very true and devoted Daikon, who graced every day of her existence, and what she was feeling no word has yet been invented for, but, oh, how her heart was beginning to shred.

Devastated, she remembered their times together, their hopes, their wishes, their dreams, all the while very much aware of the slithers closing in around her. Accepting the doom that was now inevitable, a terribly trembling Hodo shut her eyes, hoping to seek comfort in her sweet memories. Instead she found the surety of Ping's lessons waiting for her.

"Never lose sight of what you desire or where you wish to be." Ping's ethereal voice fluttered behind Hodo's eyelids.

"To live the life you deserve, you must believe that what you have on the inside can rise above any obstacle or circumstance on the outside." Ping's words came from beyond to remind her.

"There always exists two paths, the path of what is and the path of what can be. Through the choices you make and the actions you take, you can travel the path or not. It is up to you. Believe and you will achieve."

Hodo opened her eyes, giving herself over to the blessed teachings. Ping's encouragement flowed through her with a power greater than she could imagine, causing her spirit to fuse with Ping's, Ping's spirit to fuse with hers. An inner oneness of heart and mind elevated her entire being. With a renewed unity of passion and purpose to live a life divine, Hodo experienced the awakening of her will and mind. Guided by her trust in Ping's teachings, and therefore in herself, Hodo bounded the most mighty and lofty leap forward she had ever imagined, sailing into the high dark air.

Now Hodo knew nothing about slithers but she did think this: slithers can't jump. This was why the first coiling squeeze around her waist shocked her.

The second coil enveloped her upper shoulders and followed so quickly after the first that it was all part of the same awful surprise.

Now there is an instant between awareness and reality and as that instant happened, Hodo realized that no, it wasn't a slither that had her in the air. In a sky suddenly lit with stars, Hodo saw it was Ping and Daikon who had their welcoming arms firmly around her, whisking her through the perfect safety of the yellow moon's heaven. . . .

And beyond.

7

Dawn in the Mountain

Wonderment.

Daikon and Hodo had never seen a dawn like this. Looking out from the solitary grandeur of the highest mountain peak in all the land, it was a majestic vista that was beyond their conceiving. Feeling happier than they had ever been, they did what they could to control their excitement.

"Wait for it," Ping said, and he smiled.

Then it began.

Slowly at first, the intense blazing bars of molten color taking time to melt through the zenith of the upper sky. Together the three of them sat, mesmerized, their frog eyes wide with wonder at the spectacular sight. The sunrise began with a slight tinge of orange, then lit the sky with a radiant rippling scattering splendor of crimson, purple, and blue, color following color unbound as the luminous half orb rapidly grew whole, its fiery mastery of the sky taking control, revealing the panorama of a brilliant, glittering sea.

Daikon and Hodo sat with stunned astonishment, awestruck by the incredible sight. Nothing in their experience could have prepared them for the possibility of such an existence. There were no words in their vocabulary to describe the feelings they harbored inside.

Quietly, Ping pointed to the sea. "And the Great Ocean will grant each frog new hope."

Deeply moved, Daikon stared rapt at the vastness of it all. Seeing no end to the water, his eyes glistened with joyful tears. "How long has it been here?" he managed finally.

"It has been here earlier than the earliest time, and yet you cannot call it old," Ping answered. "Like yourself, it has its own unique time."

Transfixed, Hodo took in the bedazzling new world, the view drenched with tears. "In my imaginings, I knew if I went searching for something greater, I would find it."

"Whatever it is that we go searching for, it is always our self we find in the Great Ocean," said Ping. "Feel how the waves pulse with the same ecstatic rhythms of what you aspire to, for the Great Ocean is a space beyond a place, present within us all, vast and profound, ready to carry us wherever we desire to go.

"Know forever forward that for you, possibilities are as infinite as the Great Ocean is wide, such is the power of inspired purpose, the vibrant force to create the tremendous reality you wish to experience in the world."

Hodo and Daikon looked out at the fresh and flawless morning sky, experiencing the joy of existence in a new way. "I feel born again," Hodo quietly said with a look of wonder. "Everything seems so bright. In some strange way, even the sun feels different."

The greatest journey is the one you believe in.

"The greatest journey is the one you believe in," said Ping. "Perhaps your journey has taught you that the sun shines not on us, but in us."

Daikon agreed. "It is true, we have learned so much in such a short time."

"The true journey does not mark time, it merely records growth. To strive is to arrive. On the path less traveled one can come to see the light and choose to live by the light one sees. Remember your bamboo teachings; if you go as far as you can, you will discover that you can always go farther.

"You have traveled this far to find this wisdom, now you must take the journey to find yourself. Go where your great jumps take you. Embrace your decision-making power to bravely reimagine your life, and then boldly enter the stream of your destiny. Wherever you go from here, go with all your heart, knowing that every time someone finds their own way, it paves the way for others. If you knew what I know about the power of lessons learned, you would not let a single day pass without sharing it in some way. Scatter your teachings."

"With our entire being, our voices will fill the air with wisdom so that everyone may know," said Hodo.

"What you do will speak more loudly than what you say," said Ping. "This is the true knowledge of wisdom. The wise frog does not just utter words, but lives by them. The most perfect actions echo the patterns found in nature. The life of a frog is about evolving and involving. By helping to change the lives of others, yours will change, too.

"Make meaning of your beliefs, live among others, let them learn from you, start with what they know, build on what they have. Be the difference that makes the difference."

Hodo almost began to weep with gratitude. Daikon faced Ping directly. Tears glazed his eyes. He said, "Thank you for holding a light to the openness of possibility. For showing us the truth of what it is we can do with our life."

Ping looked at his fellow frogs. "I cannot show you the truth, only the way to the truth. Follow your bliss with a full heart.

The purpose of life is a life of purpose. This is the true joy, to use your life dedicated to a purpose recognized by yourself as a mighty one. Years can wrinkle a frog's skin, but to live without purpose, well, that wrinkles the soul. Always and forever, never let go of the wonder, or of your ability to let belief loose in the land."

The sudden salvation of enlightenment surrounded Daikon and Hodo. A sense of something strange flooded their hearts. At first they didn't know quite what to say. Then experiencing a blessed calm, there came just the most startling boon of realization, and it was this:

They felt no need to say anything.

No need to croak "I get...I get it," because, for the very first and most glorious time, they actually did.

Marvelous silence.

Daikon and Hodo got a blink of sunshine, felt the sky, and glanced at each other, their minds full of many things, but mainly with thoughts of their home pond and the beloved frog friends that remained behind. If only . . .

Ping took note of it all. His wizened eyes looked far out at the perfect horizon. "I can take you to the rock ravine that leads down to the Great Ocean if that is where you still wish to go," said Ping, though he knew their intent.

Daikon fingered his necklace, clutched the pond stone pendant in both hands with sweet strength. He reflected, traded glances with Hodo, and gave a soft shake of his head before he said this next: "Where we wish to go, we have already been. Hodo and I are returning home to our pond. We have promises to keep and a journey to share."

Ping's smile was never more evident. "For every beginning there is an end, and for every end a beginning. I wish you joy."

And as Daikon and Hodo gazed out at the bigger welcoming world that they now knew existed, they were contemplating only this: a journey can change the way you think about life or it can change the way you live it.

Either way, they couldn't wait to get started.

The purpose of life is a life of purpose.

Acknowledgments

In the world of storytelling, it's not news that there is always a shortage of great stories, stories that touch both the ear and the heart, the kind of stories that make you want so much to believe in the indefinable power of possibility. Sometimes there can be enlightenment so quickly. Truth be told, to have uncovered the story of Ping from such ancient stretches shrouded in mystery would not have been possible if it wasn't for those who have shared the fabulous magic of their own stories with me. Thanksgiving and cheers all for saving me a spot by the campfire: to Machiko for her stardust artistry that brings Ping wonderfully back to the surface; to everyone at Newmarket Press, especially Keith Hollaman, Executive Editor, who for years now has been the compass that keeps me on course; to Heidi Sachner, for her super savvy insight; to Harry Burton, Frank DeMaio, and Paul Sugarman for taking it from the pond to the street. To Roberto de Vicq de Cumptich, Andrea Au, Tom Peters, Guy Kawasaki, Seth Godin, and Cheryl Richardson. To Greg Horn for making a difference, Zhena Muzyka, Gerard Linsmeier, Robbin McCool, Jim Gollhofer, Darakshan Dave Farber, Gary Clow, Norm George, Tracy Stern, Barry Cooper, Paul Grabke, Erik Lukas, Ben Heins, Kurt Dommermuth, Mike Busch, Alan Wilco, and Bob Oden.

Finally, and most important: to my publisher, Esther Margolis, for always being there-there-there and who once upon a time took the time to convince me that I had ink in my veins. I was then, am still, and always will be grateful.

About the Author

Stuart Avery Gold's first book in the Ping series was *Ping: A Frog in Search of a New Pond,* an international bestseller translated into more than a dozen languages around the world, and inspired the sequel *The Way of Ping: Journey to the Great Ocean.* He is the co-author of the widely acclaimed *Success at Life; Dragon Spirit; Tiger Heart, Tiger Mind; Wowisms;* and *The Zentrepreneur's Idea Log and Workbook,* which have transformed the way people think about life and work. He is a seasoned entrepreneur and change catalyst who has dedicated his career to building socially responsible, breakthrough brands that enhance healthy living and help people achieve their best lives. His unconventional views on personal effectiveness and life mastery led CNN to label him "inspiring and energizing" and *Newsweek* to describe his energy and style as "a blend of business advice and spiritual teachings for the 21st-century entrepreneur."

Stuart was formerly the Chief Operating Officer of The Republic of Tea, which spawned the entirely new food category of specialty tea, and continues to thrive as one of the most successful specialty brands in America.

When he is not taking a breath of air in the mountains of Ojai, California, he spends his time as a guest lecturer and motivational speaker and as a consultant to companies and entrepreneurs on creativity, marketing, and innovative branding and is one of the top experts on leadership and the potential of individuals and organizations amid change.

Stuart is based in Boca Raton, Florida, and can be reached at pingthebook.com or by e-mail at info@stuartaverygold.com.

SHARE THE JOURNEY

The Way of Ping is a story of celebration that honors the past, energizes the present, and can profoundly shape the direction of your future by giving you the insights to help deal with life's daily challenges and changes effectively. Like some of the mythical heroes of old, Ping is a hero for all times, a metaphor for whatever you want in your life, a liberating invitation that urges you to see beyond your existing horizons of the familiar and comfortable into a new and more exciting way of living, by realizing your true nature and never-ending potential.

Tell us your story

The author and publisher invite you to share your thoughts and experiences about Ping and to tell us your story by contacting us at **ping@newmarketpress.com**

We hope that *The Way of Ping* has inspired you to make a leap at life's possibilities. The fact that you purchased this book proves that you are open to your limitless potential. If someone gave you this book, it proves that someone recognizes your limitless potential.